THE LEDGE

Books by Michael Collier

The Clasp and Other Poems (1986)

The Folded Heart (1989)

The Neighbor (1995)

The Ledge (2000)

Edited by Michael Collier

The Wesleyan Tradition: Four Decades of American Poetry (1993)

*The New Bread Loaf Anthology of Contemporary
American Poetry* (with Stanley Plumly) (1999)

The New American Poets: A Bread Loaf Anthology (2000)

THE LEDGE

MICHAEL COLLIER

For Dodds,
who is ready to go.

Warmest wishes,

Michael

BLWC
Aug. 17, 2005

A Mariner Book

HOUGHTON MIFFLIN COMPANY

BOSTON · NEW YORK

First Mariner Books edition 2002

For information about permission to reproduce
selections from this book, write to Permissions,
Houghton Mifflin Company, 215 Park Avenue South,
New York, New York 10003.

Visit our Web site: www.houghtonmifflinbooks.com.

Library of Congress Cataloging-in-Publication Data
Collier, Michael, date.
The ledge / Michael Collier.
    p.   cm.
ISBN 0-618-05014-0
ISBN 0-618-21910-2 (pbk.)
1. Title
PS3553.0474645 L43   2000
813'.54—dc21   99-085997

Printed in the United States of America

Book design by Victoria Hartman

DOC 10 9 8 7 6 5 4 3 2 1

Grateful acknowledgment is made to the following publications, in which these poems originally appeared: *Agni Review:* "The Word." *Alaska Quarterly Review:* "The Farrier." *Antioch Review:* "A Last Supper." *DoubleTake:* "Argos." *Gargoyle:* "Moon Valley Country Club." *Harvard Review:* "All Souls" and "Time to Move." *Kenyon Review:* "The Choice" and "My Crucifixion." *The Nation:* "A Real-Life Drama." *New England Review:* "The Hammer." *Ploughshares:* "An Awful Story," "The Blame," "Cerberus," "Safe," and "The Dolphin." *Plum Review:* "The Snake." *Seattle Review:* "Keats and Francesca." *Slate:* "The Swimmer" and "Brave Sparrow."

"The Swimmer," "Brave Sparrow," and "Pay-per-View" appeared in *The New Bread Loaf Anthology of Contemporary American Poetry,* University Press of New England, 1999.

"Ghazal" and "Ghazal of the Sahara" will appear in *Ravishing DisUnities: Real Ghazals in English,* edited by Agha Shahid Ali, Wesleyan University Press, 2000.

The author is grateful for fellowships received during the writing of this book from the John Simon Guggenheim Foundation and the University of Maryland, College Park.

For my first teachers,
Michael Moynahan, S. J.,
Anton Renna, S. J.,
and Gabriele Rico

Behind everything there is always
The unknown unwanted life

— Randall Jarrell, "The Orient Express"

CONTENTS

· III ·

ARGOS

If you think Odysseus too strong and brave to cry,
that the god-loved, god-protected hero
when he returned to Ithaka disguised,
intent to check up on his wife

and candidly apprize the condition of his kingdom,
steeled himself resolutely against surprise
and came into his land cold-hearted, clear-eyed,
ready for revenge — then you read Homer as I did,

too fast, knowing you'd be tested for plot
and major happenings, skimming forward to the massacre,
the shambles engineered with Telémakhos
by turning beggar and taking up the challenge of the bow.

Reading this way you probably missed the tear
Odysseus shed for his decrepit dog, Argos,
who's nothing but a bag of bones asleep atop
a refuse pile outside the palace gates. The dog is not

a god in earthly clothes, but in its own disguise
of death and destitution is more like Ithaka itself.
And if you returned home after twenty years
you might weep for the hunting dog

you long ago abandoned, rising from the garbage
of its bed, its instinct of recognition still intact,
enough will to wag its tail, lift its head, but little more.
Years ago you had the chance to read that page more closely

but instead you raced ahead, like Odysseus, cocksure
with your plan. Now the past is what you study,
where guile and speed give over to grief so you might stop,
and desiring to weep, weep more deeply.

SAFE

He hollowed out the book,
a window in each page,
until he made a safe
to hold the things
that made him tremble
when he touched them:
a stolen turquoise ring,
a condom sealed in foil,
a quarter lid of pot.

His house was safe and warm,
the rooms were bright occasions
and yet his dull knife
scored its way through
paragraphs and sentences
and made a steep-sided quarry
of the book, and made a joke
of the joke about books
and their covers. A need,

like any other, to hide
the self or the things
the self could not contain:
a holy card and rosary,
a boyhood picture
of his father, and a poem
typed on onionskin
and never given to the girl
who never loved him.

The boy who made this reliquary
would like to say what book
it was he carved into a heart
and made an emptiness
of a world already full:
Flight of the Phoenix,
Voyage of the Kon-Tiki?
but he can't remember, except
it was a story of adventure

and nothing like the story
of his life which was filled
with all the threats
and dangers of adventure
without adventure's thrill,
though adventure is what
he killed when he hollowed out
the book and hid the things
that made him tremble.

GHAZAL

When I was young I couldn't wait to leave home
and then I went away to make the world my home.

In England a poet's wife suggested a word for what I felt,
"*heimweh*." German for homesickness even when you're home.

The agoraphobe and claustrophobe respectively
cannot bear to leave or stay inside their home.

Our day-old son wrapped in a blanket in your arms
and I'm in the car waiting to take both of you home.

Mortgage means "dead pledge." To buy a house
you need one. A house can be mistaken for a home.

It won't be hard to name the poet who wrote a sonnet sequence
about his mother and father. He called it "The Broken Home."

A shovel, rake, and pickax hang inside my neighbor's garage.
Like a god he has ordered the chaos of his home.

Never let me forget: colliers mine coal. Michael's an angel.
In heaven as on earth the coal of grief warms the soul's home.

MY CRUCIFIXION

Not blasphemy so much as curiosity
and imitation suggested I lie faceup
and naked on my bedroom floor,
arms stretched out like His,

feet crossed at the ankles,
and my head lolling in that familiar
defeated way, while my sisters worked
with toy wooden hammers to drive

imagined spikes through my hands and feet.
A spiritual exercise? I don't think so.
For unlike Christ my boy-size penis stiffened
like one of Satan's fingers.

I was dying a savior's death and yet
what my sisters called my "thing"
struggled against extinction
as if its resurrection could not be held off

by this playful holy torture, nor stopped
except by the arrival of my parents,
who stood above us suddenly like prelates,
home early from their supper club,

stunned, but not astonished, to find
the babysitter asleep and the inquisitive
nature of our heathenish hearts amok
in murderous pageantry.

MOON VALLEY COUNTRY CLUB

After he walked through the arcadia door, almost unscathed,
like a saint, like someone materializing out of the fifth
dimension, the wall of glass parting in thousands
of deadly splinters, falling in front and behind him,
he turned to all of us watching from Tim Sawdey's
living room, and straightening himself, extended
his arms in a full benediction, hands upturned
balancing beer cans like a chalice and ciborium,
and then he bowed and curtsied. And when
he straightened again, we could see the blood
drain from his face, cheeks and lips a gravid blue,
and his legs wobbly at the knees, so that when he stepped
back through the jagged maw of the door, as if to make
the glass reassemble, the breakage heal, he collapsed
on the patio and lay in sight of us, as if he'd come
a great distance out of the fairways and traps, skirting
the water hazards, and crossing the greens to perform this trick,
and now it was time for him to lie down and sleep.

A LAST SUPPER

If I had known that leaving
guaranteed return,
I would have said good-bye

differently. I would have
got down on my knees, swept
the alley dirt into a pile,

and eaten the unforgiving grit.
I might have said, "Remember
this." Or, "Measure every future

taste, the smoke in Bucharest,
chocolate in Algeciras,
the hair and dust ingested

everywhere, against this meal
of talc and thorns." But now
that I've come back, I see

the table's set, the food's
in serving dishes, shimmering
with steam that doesn't rise.

The pewter dish, the broken-handled
cup, the fork that's like
a trident — a cutlery I bought

by never looking back—
are perfect for the meal that waits:
marble peas, carrots made

of pencil stubs, a mystery meat
of silicon—nothing you'd
ever try, unless, like me,

while you were gone
you metamorphosed—an iron jaw,
carbide teeth, graphite

skin, and fingers magnetized,
a metal hand equipped
to explore a metal wound.

Not quite the stigmata
of a saint, not quite
the evidence of restored faith.

And now, what makes me eat?
The scent of rosin, the flux that
carries solder to seal the cut.

THE WORD

"Gentlemen," the detention proctor
would begin, "you may recall Sisyphus
had a difficult life. He had to roll
a stone bigger than his own person
up a hill, et cetera, et cetera." And some
of us remembered Sisyphus from our defaced
Edith Hamiltons and some of us didn't.

Each of us deserved worse than we'd been given
for so much less than what we'd done
had been discovered. The proctor, a Jesuit,
never fit his punishments to our crimes.
"The idea of it," he said, "lacked elegance,"
though what kind of elegance he found
in a half-filled class of laggards

and reprobates I never understood, and so
we took our refresher on Sisyphus and waited
for him to assign "the word." The word—our stone—
we had to roll, neatly, as if out of a ballpoint pen,
five, six, seven hundred times.
A root ball of a word not impossible to spell
but a tangled mess to write: "Egypt," "gypsy," or "pygmy."

Unlike Sisyphus we had only an hour to complete
the task, though the proctor claimed he had
all the time in the world, until hell froze over.

Except he didn't say "hell." He said, "H–E–
double-toothpicks," as if to prove his boast
he'd never cursed, even once in his life, or as if to show

a word was the thing itself, not a stand–in
or a proctor to experience, not the near occasion
but *the* occasion. He was Christ's structuralist who doubled
as the tennis coach, whose pock-scarred face trembled
when he prayed, who saw tears of blood in Mary's marble eyes.
"H–E–double–toothpicks in a handbasket, gentlemen,"
if we didn't stifle the smirks, put our noses

to the grindstone, shoulders to the wheel, and wipe
the tarnish off the silver platter on which
we'd been handed our lives. Some of us perfected
a technique with two pens and some worked like monks
to illuminate the text with obscene hidden words.
We were subversive even as we suffered
our mild subversion, turning the torturer's delight

into the tortured's uncomfortable pleasure. We didn't know
"Jesuit" was a synonym for "sophist." We didn't know
what "sophist" meant, though now it's clear
how simple our deceptions were, our lies
like momentary lapses, and clearer still how the proctor's
skill at finding the cramp-producing words
was just a facet of a nature controlled

by a larger system of denial and forgiveness
that kept what seemed to torture him
so real it was a sin to say or spell.

THE SNAKE

A cross of oak twigs marks the place
among the ferns and ivy where the children
dug the grave and coiled the baby python
in the dirt. Why feel regret and sadness
for a thing I would not touch?
Why be anything other than annoyed about the hundred bucks
it cost, on sale! And the accessories —
glass terrarium, heating pad, thermometer,
the driftwood pedestal, the strip of AstroTurf
that lined its floor, and the sun lamp —
that cost as much. Why lament a creature
who stared down the good but nervous meal of mouse
and starved itself? Why write except to notice
how love captures love or how my wife and children
could reach inside the artificial world
and lift the serpent with their hands
and hold it like a pliable divining rod
so they could drape it over their shoulders
and laugh a creepy kind of laugh I've never laughed
as the snake constricts around their necks,
its skin a loose diamond basket weave, its shape
a necklace or a noose.

THE NEW POSSUM

Tail like a stripped turnip.
Head as narrow as a blunt carrot wedge.
This is a neighbor who knows you
better than you know yourself,
whose tongue and snout are grateful
familiars. A great eater of rats,
upholder of middle-class values,
and link to the romantic past.
It is on the frontier of biology,
a pioneer of child care. And what manners!
What an exquisite sense of its place
in the urban ecology, to appear
at night and take hold in its paws
our trash, as if it were more
than rot and spoilage,
as if it were a meal, a diet,
a sufficient content. Or the way
it lifts its head when caught
in the rake of your headlights:
a face of rubbery maquillage —
raw, plucked — a countenance
frightening and clean.

THE HAMMER

Rod of Aaron, rock sling of David,
jeweled staff of the bishop presiding
over his bishopric, Thor's weapon,
Achilles' shield — Bob Collier's hammer
bought at Walt's Hardware, near 19th Avenue

and Indian School Road, across the street
from Pete & Aggie's Double R Cocktails
and Propatti's Northwest Mortuary.
Its helve held together with electrician's tape.
The head and claw: a nose, a hook. An anvil

brought to bear on the nail or thumb — great
swearing! And lumber the saw never squared,
but made the shallow sandbox, ladder rungs up
the mulberry's V, shelves in the den. And much more
persuaded to obey the point driven home,

like a fist on a lectern — the priest, the carpenter
building their boxes of reason, a house
for the worshipful, a temple of this and that —
their pounding and pounding until the handle split,
one great fissure straight and deep. The vibration,

a current, a wrong way, refracted in the shatter,
unhealable by the hand alone. It hung like the King
of Tools from the pegboard in the service porch,
presiding over screwdrivers and pliers. Hung
in its proper place after each use until I lost it.

Lost it in the tall grass behind the fence in the alley
as I turned my attention to an ineffable problem
of existence, for what else could have provoked me
to lay down the hammer with the unpounded nails
and stand up from the pointless unaccomplished task . . .

for what? I don't remember, except later — days
or weeks — I heard my father interrogating the pegboard,
asking for his hammer. No, demanding it!
Rod of Aaron, rock sling of David. The grass in the alley
began to spark and chafe, sputter and smolder

like bad wiring. Fear put blood in my ears.
The oil of grief bleared the world to my eyes.
Deaf and blind I wandered the house and yard praying
to good St. Jude, the kind and patient Anthony, to lead me
back to the hammer and nails. My prayers

went unanswered — *Thou shall and thou shalt not* —
and my faith, unrestored, lay with the head and helve
and nails, like the lie I told my father,
and is there still in some form, rust ash and mulch
lost to my mind but incorruptible.

· II ·

A REAL-LIFE DRAMA

This dog standing in the middle of the street,
tail stiff, fur bushy with fear, and a pedigree rabbit,
its neck broken and bleeding beneath his paws,
might have been forgiven or simply taken away

and shot under different circumstances
and no one would have said much, except his owner
who'd gone out into the yard at the start
of the commotion, having been involved

at other times with the dog's truancies, and yelled,
"Bosco, Bosco, goddamnit!" but unavailing,
and everyone understanding that once more Bosco
had been taken over by the dark corner of his nature.

But this other sentiment we shared as well: the man
who'd raised the rabbit shouldn't husband something
so rare and beautiful he couldn't keep it
from the likes of Bosco.

THE SWIMMER

Nothing like him in Bosch or Breughel,
nothing so denatured as to resemble
not a semblance of a human face
but the substance of some form made
and then unmade, or like a lump
of human butter excavated from a bog.

His eyes askew, aligned by a jagged
axis that must have balanced once
across the fulcrum of his nose.
The pupils deep and lost but ever-seeing
like water in a well at night.
The head misshapen like a too-ripe

melon, dimpled by the forceps mark
of his accident or whatever extracted him
from normalcy, dipped him
in the searing, crushing waters
of disfigurement, and then returned him
to the world to fill it with the childish

worrying sound working its way
from his mouth that's not so much a mouth
as a coin purse cinched tight, sewn
with the fragments of his lips —
the yipping gait of breathlessness
he makes, which makes no sense

without the fluttering exuberance
of his hands that come to rest,
delicately, on my shoulders, as if to say:
"Help tie the drawstring of my suit,
shoulder my towel, fit these sandals
to my feet and lead me to the pool

where you will see how struggling
to be what I am, I become — otter, seal,
dolphin — released from myself, though
not absolved, not ever able to hide
the fin or the fluke, my feet
webbed and unwebbed."

THE FARRIER

The book is in my hands then his.
The desk, the lamp, the carpet fragment,
the pictures of the poets on the wall,
and then the window, and out beyond
the window, the land drops off steeply
to the river. The river winds into the sound
and the sound into the ocean. The book
we are reading is not the thing we pass
between us. The book we are reading
has not been written. It won't contain
"The Poem of Two Friends." It won't be called
"Teacher & Student," even now that one of us
is old, the other idling fluidly in middle age:
the book won't be written.
                              So how will we sort
the hammer and tongs? Who will wear
the bright bandanna around his head
or forge the useless shoe?
What is the sound the anvil
no longer makes?
                        The worked iron
cools in its own steam. It's night
beyond the window. Inside, the light
is bright enough for reading.
A mist spreads upward from the river.
The book is in his hand then mine.

for William Meredith

THE CHOICE

What does it matter,
the puddle of urine
beneath the toilet
he says he didn't make
but just discovered

and is why he called you in?
"What's this?" he asks.
"How did it get there?"
you demand. And though
there's something in his voice

that says he isn't lying,
there's no one else
near enough
for you to blame.
You've said it

many times already,
"Things don't just happen!"
And again, "How did it get that way?"
The boy wants to cry
but that would fuel

your anger, a flame,
like a pilot light,
ready to ignite. "Honesty"
is something you've tried
to instill in him,

as if to make up
for the world of lies
your life's been guided by.
And what would it hurt
for him to lie? What,

considering the choice
given him, could he do
except deny the evidence
he's brought against himself
so dutifully?

CHRISTMAS TRAIN PARK
AT THE ARBUTUS FIREHOUSE

No world has ever held so many different ways
trains operate, so many landscapes compressed
into a space no bigger than a modest living room.

No Alps as brief as these of fiberglass and papier-mâché.
No world exists planted with so many bottlebrush trees
dusted with snow, lakes of painted foil, and the town

(a ranch-house Xanadu) where a dog has caught a burglar
by the trousers as he tries to hop a privet hedge
of twist-tie loops glued in a plywood ground.

And the trains: replicas of zephyrs, the American Flyer,
speeding up and slowing down, puffs of electronic smoke,
and sleek art deco diesels like finials on skyscrapers,

or the mismatched streetcar plying a town's Main Street.
Hoppers and tankers: coal, ore and grain, oil and dairy.
Spools of cable, lumber, lathes and stamping machines

strapped like industry's colossuses across a necklace
of flatbeds, followed by boxcars with hoboes perched
in open doors, the siding codes smeared by spit.

And finally the caboose drags itself behind like a fireplace aglow,
hearth and home, an empty manger above the network
of arches and girders, the trestle spans and tunnels.

So much is going on and going on at once, so many discrete
circuits and overlays, the annual changes the firemen make,
monorail and aerial tram, like the introduction of the future,

are barely noticed. They're as static as the past of rail and tie
and spike — what once was the wide becoming of America —
but now, along with models of civics, the human scale of
          hardware stores,

they're left behind. What remains beside the alarms warning
of the town's ceaseless fires is illumined by the printed dials
and gauges no one sees except the engineers of lead and plastic,

who watch, as we watch, the world repeat itself.

THE LESSONS

1

At first you think he's ogling you or someone
at the urinal but the way he shifts his weight
and stares at the tile between the toilets and showers
he seems to be waiting patiently, but then he starts
to pace along the bank of sinks and mirrors,
mumbling and lisping as if he's reminding himself
of something unforgettable, a list he can't quite keep
inside his head, and so he speaks his mind?

But that's not what it is. That's not what finally
makes him call, "Jeff?" and "Jeffrey!" His voice plaintive
then pleading. "Jeff?" and "Jeffrey!" as if they were
different names for the same person and not the lisp
and mumble of his pacing but the What? What now!
of a duty he can never relinquish. So just as he begins
to call again, a toilet stall bangs open and a boy,
who must be Jeffrey, shuffles out, swimsuit snagged

at his knees, a wad of paper in his hand, a blossom
held out to his father, who uses it to wipe his son.

2

Forty years ago when you learned to swim
your mother led you to the threshold of the boys' room,
a cool cement floor, the smell of urine under bleach,
cigarette butts in the urinal, no mirrors, a clogged sink —

a vestibule of terror choked with clothes and shoes,
and on the other side, those who made it sat on the pool's edge
while the instructor, waist deep like a centaur, strode up
and down the line of dangling legs and ordered you to kick

and splash. He didn't seem to care that you screamed—
but the one or two who hadn't yet emerged,
whose mothers called their names with so much sympathy
you wished you'd been as brave, them the instructor
began to scold as if he were their fathers fed up
with the shame a son brings being frightened
of the ordinary world. And so they arrived, the one or two,
screaming a different kind of scream, and what they learned

was not to swim so much as how to keep from drowning
and what followed when you stopped responding to your name.

CATBIRD

Was it late summer evening
when the bird sang or early dawn,
when the mind is like a bird's
late summer evening song?

No one remembers, though the child asks,
"What was the bird called
who sang that night, sang
all summer long?"

ALL SOULS

A few of us — Hillary Clinton, Vlad Dracula,
Oprah Winfrey, and Trotsky — peer through
the kitchen window at a raccoon perched
outside on a picnic table where it picks

over chips, veggies, olives, and a chunk of pâté.
Behind us others crowd the hallway, many more
dance in the living room. Trotsky fusses with the bloody
screwdriver puttied to her forehead.

Hillary Clinton, whose voice is the rumble
of a bowling ball, whose hands are hairy
to the third knuckle, lifts his rubber chin to announce,
"What a perfect mask it has!" While the Count

whistling through his plastic fangs says, "Oh,
and a nose like a chef." Then one by one
the other masks join in: "Tail of a gambler,"
"a swashbuckler's hips," "feet of a cat burglar."

Trotsky scratches herself beneath her skirt
and Hillary, whose lederhosen are so tight they form a codpiece,
wraps his legs around Trotsky's leg and humps like a dog.
Dracula and Oprah, the married hosts, hold hands

and then let go. Meanwhile the raccoon squats on
the gherkins, extracts pimentos from olives, and sniffs
abandoned cups of beer. A ghoul in the living room
turns the music up and the house becomes a drum.

The windows buzz. "Who do you love? Who do you love?"
the singer sings. Our feathered arms, our stockinged legs.
The intricate paws, the filleting tongue.
We love what we are; we love what we've become.

TIME TO MOVE

Good intentions were always saving him
from himself, from his neighbors,
and from his neighbors' wives,
who in the climate of the times
became more his friends than his wife's,

but adultery was the smallest of temptations,
the least threat to him and his wife,
or so they thought, though it certainly
was one of the many things held
in abeyance while they kept filling

the rented house with other threats.
The long absences in time and place
from each other, absences that were
states of mind, so that even while
he slept next to her, he occupied

some other place where close by
a suitcase lay open and inside
the contents arranged like the instruments
of his diplomacy: a pocket reading light
for the train, slippers, ear plugs,

a small pillow for his back — accouterments
of the sick, and the rooms he occupied
while away, his office and basement
sleeping den, like places for the sick.
Though he wasn't sick exactly.

He'd made the stoic's choice to keep
his heart and counsel in his suitcase,
hour by hour, time to move, to have
a destination, modes of conveyance,
to be happy, though to take no pleasure,

to be an ambassador to his different selves,
shuttling from place to place,
and all of this so he could feed the anger
of his decision, his choice, which he stacked
and restacked like a rick waiting for a match.

A REMAINDER

Arrhythmia was the title of the book. *Arrhythmia
and Other Stories.* A glossy black dust jacket
with a complicated holographic heart as vivid
as a picture of anatomy in the *World Book of Knowledge,*

compounded by overlays of plastic where staticky
transparency could be peeled from staticky transparency
until you reached the heart's core — a huge necktie knot
of muscle. The book stacked with others on a cart

of dollar bargains outside a shop where I stopped
to kill time. A name is so much harder to remember
than a face, a face is so much language compressed.
The author's name stamped in gold beneath the textured,

naked heart meant nothing until the jacket photograph,
a head shot, sprung out from the inside flap unfolding
in my hand, as if I'd caught an energy the book
could not contain — a face and name now clearly printed

in bold type with facts about her life: her name a plant,
a vine with tiny feet that grows on anything, spade-
shaped leaves, green and black-veined, but not
the name I knew her by twenty years ago, the one

she'd given to herself, not a name really but an assault
on her name, an activity spelled out in scars
across her stomach and down her thighs, not imperfections
of skin as first I'd thought, not anything at my age then

I could imagine or easily comprehend or not doubt
except when she said how only recently she'd stopped
cutting herself. "I'm a bleeder," she said. And that's
the name I've thought of through the years when

I've thought of her. The razor that made her feel
both better and worse about herself. "Worse," she said,
because you could not respect the inch of suicide each slash
defined and "better" because at last you'd done something

to confirm your utter worthlessness. Now, it seems ridiculous.
But her book, which I found by accident, is evidence
she survived, that we survived! A young woman in one
          of her stories
asks a character named White Boy, "Tell me, am I beautiful?"

And he responds, "No, not beautiful, but exotic," which was
          another way
I had for saying lovely, baffling, and all-consuming,
everything White Boy could never be except in proximity
to the danger she embodied: the bleeder, self-named, and
          that other name —

the vine whose leaves were shaped like hearts, not spades.

THE WAVE

Vendors with racks of soft drinks, palettes
of cotton candy, ice cream in bright insulated
bags, pretzels in metal cabinets, and the peanut
man with his yellow peanut earring. Money folded

between fingers, spokes of green waving
in the glad pandemonium greeting the Budman
with his quick-pouring mechanism strapped
to his wrist like a prosthesis, or the hotdog guy

genuflecting in the steep aisles, anointing
the roll and weenie with mustard before passing
it down to the skinny kid sitting between fat parents.
In the air above us the flittering birds, attracted

and repelled by planetary field lights, swoop
in ecstatic arcs, trapped under a dark invisible dome.
The park organ, the JumboTron, the mascot
pacing atop the visitors' dugout, taunting them

with oversize antics, while the groundskeepers
mist the infield with a fire hose, leavening
the calm, raked earth . . . Later, in the fifth
or sixth, two soldiers sitting next to me, who

have paced each other with a beer an inning and kept
their buzz buffed with a flask, take off their shirts,
though the night's cool, and move to the front row,
where they face the crowd, sweep up their arms,

and command us to rise from our seats.
At first only a few respond, but like molecules quickening
or cells dividing or herds stampeding, we coalesce —
orison provoking unison — section by section, as if

township by township, our standing up and sitting down
becomes the Simon Says and Mother May I? of a nation,
as it runs through our rippling, shimmering, upraised hands
that form the crest of a wave built on the urges

and urgings of the soldiers, whose skin is slick with sweat
or some other labor and whose goal now, for all of us,
for themselves, for the players on the field, is simply to stay
in the wave, to keep it going for as long as they can.

BRAVE SPARROW

whose home is in the straw
and baling twine threaded
in the slots of a roof vent

who guards a tiny ledge
against the starlings
that cruise the neighborhood

whose heart is smaller
than a heart should be,
whose feathers stiffen

like an arrow fret to quicken
the hydraulics of its wings,
stay there on the metal

ledge, widen your alarming
beak, but do not flee as others have
to the black walnut vaulting

overhead. Do not move outside
the world you've made
from baling twine and straw.

The isolated starling fears
the crows, the crows gang up
to rout a hawk. The hawk

is cold. And cold is what
a larger heart maintains.
The owl at dusk and dawn,

far off, unseen, but audible,
repeats its syncopated intervals,
a song that's not a cry

but a whisper rising from concentric
rings of water spreading out across
the surface of a catchment pond.

It asks, "Who are you? Who
are you?" but no one knows.
Stay where you are, nervous, jittery.

Move your small head a hundred
ways, a hundred times, keep
paying attention to the terrifying

world. And if you see the robins
in their dirty orange vests
patrolling the yard like thugs,

forget about the worm. Starve
yourself, or from the air inhale
the water you may need, digest

the dust. And what the promiscuous
cat and jaybirds do, let them
do it, let them dart and snipe,

let them sound like others.
They sleep when the owl sends
out its encircling question.

Stay where you are, you lit fuse,
you dull spark of saltpeter and sulfur.

· III ·

PAY-PER-VIEW

Maybe you saw this as I did in a smoke-free
suite of the Allard Hotel in Chicago,
late in the afternoon, an hour away from drinks,
then dinner with a friend, after a long day of meetings.

Like me you clicked on the TV, surfed through
weather, CNN, and local news before stopping
at a woman with hair the color
of embalming fluid — a rose hips red.

She held up a pheasant by its legs in one hand
and a chicken in the same fashion with the other.
Both of the birds had been decapitated, plucked,
maybe even oiled, for they shone and glistened.

The pheasant was longer, leaner than the chicken
and, through the sheen, its skin was a whitish-gray
like asphalt dusted with snow. The chicken, robust,
jaundice-colored, hung swollen and fat. The woman placed

each fowl on its own large cutting board. A row of knives
lay waiting, but before she began dressing the birds
I changed channels, once, twice, and then rapidly,
turning the screen into a flip book, a cavalcade of images:

the U.S. Congress, a diamond necklace rotating in mid-air,
a bowling ball smashing silently into pins, and Lotto numbers,
as if they were verses of apocrypha, flashed above a blowup of
a check made out to *John Doe* for *Thirty Million Dollars and No
    One Hundredths.*

Occasionally the screen filled with bands of houndstooth or plaid,
scrambled colors behind which figures moved and a steady droning
music played, the kind the Harpies might have made for Sisyphus
each time he reached the hilltop. Beneath the music

and behind the meadowy zippers of color, I heard moaning,
a held-in keening, and staring hard, trying to locate
the sound in the bright reticulating light, I saw a man morph
his head long, Martian green, arms without hands, legs

as malleable as mercury and then, as if engrafted to him or giving
birth to his form and deformation, a woman. Zeus made Pandora
from clay and had the four Winds fill her with life. She was not
a real woman but a god's vengeful fantasy of beauty.

And now those winged souls that once escaped
from her exquisite jar — the shadows of our pains, the venom
carriers of our desires — assemble an erotic chaos on the screen.
Delusive hope, which grows the liver back from the shreds

and tatters of the demons' feeding, entered me as perhaps
it enters you — a dryness in the throat, a conviction fed by
a yearning that in time the obscure and pleasure-giving bodies
would emerge clear and free.

CERBERUS

He was the yard dog's yard dog.
His heads accessorized with snakes.
His tail a scorpion's, and his slaver
a seed bank for hell's herbarium.
And his bites were worse than his barks.

What did he do in the underworld
except to guard the stairs leading
from the bitter tide-lap of the Styx?
How did he spend his days in the darkness
where only the dead can see?

His rheum-yellow eyes. His chainmail ears
larger than a basset's. Slower than Charon
at sorting the dead from the living—
yet more accurate, for like the dog
he was, he knew the various scents from the world above:

the grasses and tree bark, scat tracks,
the sweet acrid talc of dried piss. He knew
the dirt-under-the-nail smell of the desperate digging
from the buried-alive, the iron-on-the-tongue
of the licked wound. As ugly as he was,

he had exquisite breeding, a species unto himself.
The stud who would never have a mate. His cock,
a huge suppurating rudder, stirred the sulfuric
ocean of his realm; a homing device like his anger,
uncircumcised, guiding, probing, a love that could kill.

SWANS

Tamed, stuffed, but once alive, they are the huge fear
of my clumsy body: the stilled arms, thick unusable wings,
legs like rusted rebar. But now as we press closer

to the glass display and the strange, almost-speckled
reflections of smaller birds hover in the air behind us,
each species profiled and paired — what would I do

if you took my hand and held it? Instead you move past me,
and as I turn to follow, after so many years together,
I'm still unsure of the right interval to keep between us

or even what unit to measure the distance — paces or seconds?
In a hall of dioramas I catch up with you: savannah,
desert, and woodland, where the creatures blend

with their habitat, and where even eyes as trained as ours
to watch the hidden, camouflaged markings of moods, study hard
to find the tree frogs and moths, songbirds and snakes who survive

by taking on the shape and color of their world.

HUMMINGBIRD AVIARY

Scarlet and teal
raven and maize
throat-blush
and wing-strobe.

Breathless stutter, vertigo,
feint, heart-frenzy,
small skitterings,
stalled vectors.

Bodies like thumbs,
syringe nose, flick-birr
of wings, blur
of invisible air.

A tongue and a taste
the one and the other
a claustrophobe's panic
now quivering, now calm.

GHAZAL OF THE SAHARA

When I turned to say something the presence was gone.
Sand in the palm of an open hand is an essence gone.

The road ended. I found the map was untrue or the sand
had shifted. When will I find where the lost road's gone?

Blink of an eye — Thursday in Douz and the market is busy;
Bedouins dressed like Old Testament shepherds — and the
       present is gone.

Of course, it's true, the Sahara's an ocean, waves of sand —
but look, I dip in my hand and the ocean is gone.

Rose crystals blossom in Chott el Djerid, the sand's crude
sculpture rising where the water rises, a mirage, and then is gone.

Phoenix dactylifera, a poet's tree! *Doigts de lumière*.
I hold my hand up to block the sun and the sun is gone.

Quicksand? Don't struggle, move slowly, the guidebook
reports; it takes hours before you're completely gone.

When the desert inside me matched the nothingness beyond,
I recited my name, and the presence was gone.

LONG SUMMER

The bee is mad for light
and like the moth it tries
to penetrate the window.
When it succeeds, the madness
brought inside intensifies:
head banger in fierce
autistic flight, an orbit
from which it drops
half broken to the desk,
legs paddling the air,
wings rowing the black
lacquer of its surface,
and even so, its eyes,
faceted, stereo-
metric, provoked by light.
And madness spurred
by incapacity
changes key — a rattle,
a jew's-harp twang and buzz,
electric quivering,
except the moth whose wings
and fuselage leak dust.

in memoriam, Ben Branch

FATHOM AND LEAGUE

Two miles down the sea floor is a skull,
the wounded head of a monster — fractured,
faulted, ridged. It won't make me think
of the earth as Mother or understand Gaea,

but that my heart is inside my body
and neutral buoyancy is good. How else
can the world be studied? But if life begins
in the ocean, it thrives on hot and cold,

in the tumble and boil of the sea no longer silent.
In genesis there's no happiness, only awe
and improbability. The hideous is beautiful:
worms ten feet long, clams the size of Frisbees,

and shrimp that swarm like insects. And something else:
water burning inside of water, smoking spires
and chimneys. And here and there, to calibrate
and measure, a weighted buoy, a probe or camera

I'm coming to retrieve. The sonar pings
as if it had an ear to my heart. The echo
coming back goes through and doesn't stop
until it dissipates, a question formed of sound,

empty of the shapes it failed to find beyond
the submarine's perimeter of light. Now
at the site of the world's making and unmaking
the way to stay intact is to remain inside the sphere

as if it were a choice I'd made to define myself,
but it's no choice. The hatch is held in place
by the weight of 300 atmospheres: sky upon sky.
There's no courage in this safety, no danger

in this passing. The data siphoned, the vents named
Godzilla, Hulk, Inferno. My metaphor of monster?
The figure of fathom, measuring the depths, holding
the unseen dark close, hearing in it the sound

of its own shape — a name, then a creature, an issue,
made of what I hold, and nothing more,
the span, fingertip to fingertip, of an embrace.

for John Delaney

THE BLAME

That which you made me do I did.
That which you made me say I said.
Now the blame, like oil over water,
spreads, and so our life together
that began in vows — the licensed oath —
has leased itself back to us both:
what we knew and couldn't know
what our words no longer show.

AN AWFUL STORY

When she came into his room he was asleep
and when she touched him, he woke —
her hand on his shoulder, her knee at his mouth,
and in the darkness, she looked like a boy.

When he tried to sit up she covered his ears
with her hands: "Save ourselves from ourselves,"
she said, and then a wind stirred in the room
as if she'd placed those words in his mouth.

ALL DARKNESS

All darkness at the back of the service porch,
darkness and apprehensiveness in making out shapes
from shadows, what even now he fears to put his hand into —
the nothingness of night that is the lightless space
of a room or cupboard, a glove box without its tiny bulb.

The undelineated, guessed at, groped for, and missed
that becomes, in the realm of light, the untried,
his held-back-from of all fear's fear. But not this
greater darkness of the other: sheet-shaped, near
to hand and, when the hand touches, trembling or disturbed.

THE DOLPHIN

When the fin of faithlessness appeared
I watched it circle, dip and veer
then ride the swells. Where I stood,

on shore among the surf casters' gear,
RVs and 4x4s, I tried to guess
where it would rise, sleek bottlenose

breaking next, so I might measure
the erratic progress that it made
beyond the haunting thought that hung

in me, and so ten years married
to the sleek warm thigh of that image,
I reached out — my hand pointing toward

the turbulence — and tried holding on
to what revealed itself as only something
passing by. But years are distance

and outside their measurement
is a circumference in which knowledge
circulates, a current of otherness,

vortex and siphon, the place where
the water spout returns to the ocean,
toward which we call out to a wife

or husband who now beyond the safety
of the shore hears that voice
which might turn them from their frenzy.

KEATS AND FRANCESCA

The melancholy storm. The clouds
metropolitan. How was the wire
to stretch across the ocean?
The white egg placed against the white door?

In a dream words unraveled
and an ungloved hand touched him.
His attention marred. The flawed rain.
The hailstones. The descent

into wild darkness and wild darkness
descending. City of clouds.
Kingdom of moods. You need not tell your sorrow.
Lightning caught in the fabric of his coat.

PAX GEOLOGICA

Last night the world's rifts, the ridges
that lie under the oceans, entered my dream,
seams and wounds of creation that spread
and subduct, whose monumental movement
makes mountains, erupts volcanoes,
and sets continents adrift.

In that peaceful destruction the possessions
of our house lay scattered on the floor
like a collection of basalt, glassine,
brittle from cooling, shaped like pillows
and sheets and columns from the temple
of the world's beginnings.

But out beyond the talus walls, over the caldera's edge,
the earth's manufacture of abyss slipped by
slowly. That was the night's upwelling, and in it
the sheer transparent creatures coalesced,
rafts of stellar luminescence — red, blue, and green —
deep, beyond reach, but in the world.

ABOUT THE AUTHOR

MICHAEL COLLIER has been the director of the Bread Loaf Writers' Conference for five years and has taught English at the University of Maryland, College Park, for fifteen years. His previous volumes of poetry are *The Clasp and Other Poems, The Folded Heart,* and most recently *The Neighbor.* Collier is the recipient of a Guggenheim fellowship, NEA fellowships, and the Discovery/*The Nation* Award, among other honors.